Redleaf *Quick* Gui

Developmental Milestones

OF YOUNG CHILDREN

Karen Petty, PhD

Redleaf Press®
www.redleafpress.org
800-423-8309

Published by Redleaf Press
10 Yorkton Court
St. Paul, MN 55117
www.redleafpress.org

First edition 2010 by Redleaf Press
Interior typeset in Univers
Printed in the United States of America
17 16 15 14 13 12 11 10   2 3 4 5 6 7 8 9

Library of Congress Cataloging-in-Publication Data

Petty, Karen.
 Developmental milestones of young children / Karen Petty.
   p. cm. — (Redleaf quick guide)
 ISBN 978-1-60554-005-4 (alk. paper)
 1. Child development—Handbooks, manuals, etc. I. Title.
 HQ767.9.P475 2009
 305.231—dc22
            2009009664

Printed on acid-free paper

To my grandsons, Kason, Jay, Sam, and Zaidon, who have brought me more joy than I ever imagined and whose stages of development instructed and inspired my writing throughout this book.

Developmental Milestones of Young Children

Introduction

Karen Petty, PhD

Benchmarks of development are important to all caregivers and families alike because they provide information that can help them both observe and chart a child's development over time. While environments, child-to-adult ratios, caregiving routines, and group size are important for young children in care, knowledge of and attention to children and their development are most important. This book provides descriptions of developmental milestones, which are behaviors exhibited by children (and observed by caregivers) at certain times during their development from infancy through early school age.

How to Use This Book

This book can be used as a caregiver's guide to the typical developmental milestones of children ages birth through eight years. This book is *not* a diagnostic tool or a remedy for children with developmental delays or differing abilities. The book is intended as a quick reference that can be used alone or in conjunction with the Developmental Milestones Observational Record, which can be downloaded from the Redleaf Press Web site (www.redleafpress.org). Type *developmental milestones* into the Search Catalog box, and follow the links.

Who Is This Book For?

Parents frequently ask, "How will I know if my baby is progressing normally?" or "Is my baby keeping up with other kids his age?" The more caregivers know about young children and their stages of development, the less anxious and better prepared they are to care for children at any age or stage. Caregivers of young children—teachers, child care providers, families, and friends—will benefit from this book because the valuable information it contains will help them understand and know when a young child may need special care or diagnostics. While no measure of development can be considered definitive, some typical milestones are achieved universally by most children at particular ages and stages. Knowing that children develop along a continuum that is unique to each individual child, caregivers can use these general milestones to identify when a child may be developing slower than average.

Why Study the Development of Children?

The more caregivers know about the children in their care, the better they will be able to provide appropriate experiences for them. Noticing behaviors such as an infant smiling when she hears a particular voice or a preschooler getting cranky each day after mealtime will give caregivers a sense of who the child really is. Small observances such as these further caregivers' knowledge of child development and their familiarity with and understanding of the children in their care.

The Caregiver and Development

To be a professional in the field of child development and the care of young children, an understanding of the children in care is crucial. Caregivers need to understand the domains of child development as well as the behaviors typical of children at a particular age. This book can be used as a source of information for families and others who care for children. As caregivers learn more and more about children and developmental milestones, their individual planning for each child will improve.

Diversity

Caregivers can make efforts to celebrate the diversity of children as members of a family unit and as individuals with specific characteristics that are all their own. Children are one-of-a-kind and unique in their own ways. They come from families who represent diverse cultures, languages, abilities, and experiences. It is the caregiver's job to learn about each child's background in order to know each child in a more sensitive and meaningful way.

Knowing the child means knowing the family, and connections to families can be made stronger and more meaningful when caregivers take the time to bring the diversity of families' lives into their own practice. After all, caregivers share the same goal with each family—for their child to succeed.

Domains of Development

There are many domains of development, but this book focuses on four:

- physical/motor development

- social/emotional development

- language development

- cognitive development

Each domain is important in its own right but also works in tandem with the others. Children do not function in a single domain at a time. As children carry out their daily tasks, they often work in several or all of the domains concurrently. The four domains listed above are addressed for each age and each developmental stage throughout this book. They can look dramatically different from one age to the next. For example, a child's vocabulary skills at one year are dramatically different from a child's vocabulary skills at eight years. The domains help categorize the observed behaviors and milestones.

Karen Petty, PhD, holds a master's degree in early childhood education and a doctorate in curriculum and instruction with emphases in early childhood and child development. She has over twenty years of experience teaching and caring for young children and conducting trainings and workshops. Dr. Petty is a consultant for military installation family member programs and is the author of *Deployment: Strategies for Working with Kids in Military Families*. She is an associate professor in early childhood development and education at Texas Woman's University in Denton, Texas.

Chapter 1: Observing Children

Observation is probably the best way to assess and document developmental milestones in young children. It takes skill to become an accomplished observer, but you as a caregiver can better understand children—their behaviors, skills, knowledge, and feelings—if you watch and listen to them in focused and purposeful ways. The more you observe, the more you become aware of each child's unique abilities. As you conscientiously watch and listen to children, you can record what you observe and document development. In addition to revealing much about children and their development, ongoing, focused observations can keep you centered on each individual child rather than only on those whose behaviors frequently command your attention. Observation is also an authentic way to systematically record children's behavior.

The Developmental Milestones Observational Record, which can be used with this book, is a good resource to help you maintain your focus, know what to look for, and know when each milestone may occur.

You can download a PDF of the Developmental Milestones Observational Record from the Redleaf Press Web site. Go to www.redleafpress.org, type *developmental milestones* into the Search Catalog box, and follow the links.

The Developmental Milestones Observational Record will help you maintain good documentation of a child's development over time. By using the observational record, your biases will be minimized because you will be concentrating on observing certain behaviors and skills rather than on trying to interpret what you see. That is, instead of trying to interpret a child's behavior, you will simply record whether the child is in the *learning* stage of development, the *practicing* stage, or the *mastery* stage based on your observations.

The learning stage occurs when a child is experiencing something for the first time or when a task is initially being taught. For example, by six months most babies can transfer a toy from one hand to another. You can purposefully refer to the observational record and offer opportunities for children to work toward each milestone. In this way, the observational record becomes an excellent planning tool. You can use your recorded observations to plan developmentally appropriate events for the children in your care.

Children are in the practicing stage when they have been exposed to a new skill but haven't quite mastered it. You as the caregiver or teacher should continue to provide the children with opportunities for learning the skill until they reach an "aha" moment and perform the skill or behavior on their own. Observing as a way of developing and facilitating curriculum is more appropriate than using curriculum that may be unrelated to the developmental stages of the particular children in your care or that may be based on skills or themes that aren't particularly relevant.

The mastery stage comes when children have consistently performed or exhibited a behavior over a period of time without your assistance. For example, it would be premature to record mastery for the milestone "stands alone" if a one-year-old attempted to stand unassisted on one occasion and then did not attempt to stand alone for another month.

The observational record is an authentic assessment tool that may be more appropriate for early childhood settings than formal assessments, which tend to take a snapshot of a child's behavior or ability during a single incident. Using the observational record allows caregivers an opportunity to conveniently observe the child more than once and over time. It also allows more than one person to make an observation and to record what is observed, which provides greater validity to and consistency in the child's records. The most important reason to observe children, however, is to benefit them personally by providing their caregivers and families a holistic look at their development in several domains over time, rather than in just one specific area at one specific time.

Observation done informally in real settings may be the best way to chart children's progress, or lack thereof. It can be used to give information about the development of the children in your care as well as to provide information about how well the children are progressing toward the outcomes or standards of your program. Your curriculum can be built on the authentic assessments you do with the children during their daily routines—indoor and outdoor play, group times, and learning activities—rather than in pullout testing and measurement situations or through standardized testing. The best observations for assessment of young children

- are based on knowledge of children and their development;
- occur over time;
- look at children individually as well as with other children;
- are done by the child's caregiver or teacher;
- are based on strengths rather than weaknesses;
- are performance based;
- include samples of a child's speech or work.

How to Use the Observational Record

The developmental milestones found in the observational record are important events in the lives of young children ages birth through eight years. They reflect the current understanding of children's growth and development. Along with the benefits discussed previously, the observational record can also provide an alert if a child is in need of additional or more in-depth assessments by outside observers, such as diagnosticians, doctors, and consultants. As the observational record is used for activity planning and assessment, remember that the ages associated with each milestone are expected rather than definite. No child develops at the same rate as others. When using the observational record

- try to be discreet;
- observe during routines and activities;
- focus on a single domain of development at a time rather than trying to complete the whole checklist at once;
- concentrate on one child at a time;

- plan activities that foster behaviors and skills on the observational record;

- avoid making judgments or inferences about a child (be as unbiased and objective as possible);

- listen for words that are said and record them in the observational record.

The observational record can display a lot of information at a glance that is easy to understand and interpret. Adults other than the observer/recorder can use the information to continue to track a child's progress. The records can be passed on to future caregivers in a child's portfolio. The observational record, along with samples of the child's work, gives a true picture of the growth and development of the whole child.

Chapter 2: Documenting Milestones

Learning about children comes from careful observations—listening to and watching children in authentic environments. You can become a skilled observer who studies children and documents the important milestones they achieve over time. Documenting milestones is a two-step process: (1) collecting the information that is observed, and (2) recording it.

Your collection of information about young children should be based on focused observations of appropriate developmental milestones. The developmental milestones listed in the observational record can be used to guide your observations.

Recording what you observe is important, because it becomes a written record of the child's performance. It also allows you to save valuable information in a way that can be easily referenced; that is, you don't have to rely on your memory to know what the child can do. Based on the child's prior performance, you can create authentic activity plans rather than using a theme of the day or other "cute" ideas that have no basis in a child's developmental stage. This written record will also be a valuable tool when communicating with families.

Documentation can be used to show a child's progress through the stages on the developmental continuum—learning, practicing, and mastery—and can show patterns of growth such as sitting up, crawling, and walking in infants, or scribbling, controlled drawing, and writing in preschoolers. Additional benefits for documenting observed behaviors include

- assuring families you are committed to providing care based on the needs of their children;

- organizing the observations;

- putting an emphasis on learning and development;

- expanding learning to higher-level thought processes;

- challenging the child to develop or extend skills;

- increasing your ability as a professional.

You can share your documentation of a child's progress with families during conferences and scheduled or impromptu meetings. Just knowing you conduct purposeful and focused observations for documenting purposes is reassuring and exciting to families interested in the continuing development of their child.

Systematically recording observations on particular days of the week and when events occur can help you organize your observations. The emphasis of documentation should be on learning and development—looking at a child's strengths instead of weaknesses.

The observational record is organized by the four domains of development covered in this book—physical/motor, social/emotional, language, and cognitive. It provides a list of the milestones typically achieved in

- the first year of life;

- one-year-olds;

- two-year-olds;

- three-year-olds;

- four-year-olds;

- five-year-olds;

- six-year-olds;

- seven-year-olds;

- eight-year-olds.

Attention is given to each domain of development during each of the first nine years of life in order to assess the whole child rather than only one facet of the child. As you observe, you may find patterns of development. For example, you may observe that three-year-old Kya shows advanced language ability but not advanced physical/motor skills. This does not mean she won't someday excel in the physical/motor tasks; it just shows that at this stage in her development, she has achieved the mastery stage in the language domain while being at the practice stage in her physical/motor domain. It is important to document a child's ability over time by doing multiple observations. Completing the record of three observations each year is advised, though you may wish to do more observations if you think them necessary.

Not all of the domains have equal numbers of milestones to observe and record due to natural patterns of development found in children on the whole. For example, in the "birth to one year" category, the physical/motor development domain has many more observable milestones than do the other three domains. This isn't surprising, considering the extreme amount of physical/motor development that occurs during the first year of a child's life. If you care for infants, your observations and documentations will probably occur more often, but they may not be more demanding to conduct given the limited mobility of the children, the smaller caregiving spaces, and the smaller group sizes.

When caring for children without a focus on documenting milestones, we often see and watch children carefully, but we do not necessarily observe them. As you familiarize yourself with the observational record for the ages of children in your care, you may begin to observe milestones you didn't notice when you were just watching. Over time, observation and documentation will become easier (if not automatic) as milestones are encountered. Your documentation should include narratives using quotes from the children, objective comments from the observers, and other anecdotal information.

As you provide activities for the children in your care, make efforts toward increasing the children's learning to higher-level thought processes. Whenever possible, scaffold (or assist) children when they learn new tasks in order to move them toward practicing them and then eventually to mastering them.

An added benefit that naturally occurs when you use an observational record is the expansion of your abilities as a professional. Your children benefit, and you benefit, too, as you become more knowledgeable of young children and the milestones important for them to achieve.

Recording Observations through Documentation

Some caregivers keep clipboards nearby in order to make quick recordings of behaviors, and some use sticky notes to jot down observed skills or abilities. Others use index cards stuffed in apron pockets or charts posted behind cabinet doors to capture moments when children accomplish firsts. Still others plan activities around particular skills and have the observational record handy to document comments about the children and dates of observations. No matter what recording method you decide to use, a thorough understanding of the observational record prior to observing will make recording events easier. You may focus for a day on reporting one child's progress toward several milestones, or you may document a particular milestone for a group of children at once, such as "child skips with two feet" for all of the older preschoolers and young schoolagers in your care. You can devise your own systematic way of observing and documenting the achievement of milestones, but what is most important is finding one or several methods that work best for you as an individual. *You* know when *you* can best observe and record the actions of the children in your care.

Chapter 3: Communicating with Families

Documenting milestones has a direct benefit for families as you observe, record, and share a child's progress. Quality care uses observation and documentation of children's abilities at its core. With an increased public awareness of good programs for young children, including infants and toddlers, your efforts to provide records of children's progress over time is vital to family communication and relationships. The best programs for young children are based on strong commitments to and partnerships with families, and this book offers much in the way of building those relationships.

The observational record can become an important document for you and children's families. As you share the observational record with families, they too can become empowered to observe their own children in ways that go beyond merely watching. Whether your care is center or home based, you can involve families in the overall developmental milestones documentation process.

Partnerships with Families

Seek partnerships with families as you assess children's development through the observational record. Communicate your observations and assessments of milestones with families, and listen to families' stories. Share photos, art, drawings, narratives, anecdotes, and stories with families, and encourage families to share the same with you. When families perceive themselves as equal partners with caregivers, they are much more apt to participate in the assessment process. For example, you might say, "I'm seeing James getting up on all fours. It looks like he is preparing to crawl. Are you seeing this at home as well?" Meetings with families can become celebrations of what their children *can do.* Assure families that your purpose is not to diagnose but to share ways their children are growing and developing over time.

Two-Way Communication with Families

A mutual exchange of information regarding children's development between families and you, the caregiver, is much more advantageous than the traditional one-way exchange, where the caregiver does all the talking while the families listen. This isn't communicating. Families are valuable resources when it comes to their children, and it is commonly known that children benefit from positive relationships between their families and caregivers.

Maintaining an open dialogue can give much insight into children's development and can assist in the observation and documentation of milestones. While keeping the information gained through observation discreet and adhering to the ethics of privacy for each child, you can find ways to communicate effectively with families. The following are some common and popular forms of two-way communication:

- family-teacher conferences (scheduled, impromptu, or as necessary)

- phone calls from families to caregivers and from caregivers to families (scheduled and unscheduled)

- arrival and departure conversations (with discretion)

To help families understand the observational record, you can schedule a conference with each family to review the record and to let them know what you will be observing and recording throughout the year. Or you may want to plan an evening gathering where all families are invited to attend a tutorial that will guide them through the observational record. That way, all families can hear the same information and have the opportunity to ask questions and make comments or suggestions. Either way, families will be better informed and, as a result, may take steps to foster the skills required of their children to meet each milestone. Share the observational record with families so they, too, can chart their child's performance in the home environment, and provide opportunities for sharing your observations along with theirs as you work together to support efforts. Families will welcome education in order to provide guidance and opportunities for children's skills to emerge at home. This united support system will benefit both caregivers and families and, most important, the children.

Bringing Up Concerns

After carefully tracking children's behavior and development, you may begin to observe patterns that suggest developmental delays. Perhaps you have concerns regarding one or more domains of development. This book can help you describe children's typical development to families and express where a child is on the developmental continuum at a given point in time. Families depend on caregivers to monitor children's progress and to alert them of concerns. On the other hand, caregivers should not make specific diagnoses or give advice about truly problematic behaviors. If growth is not occurring, you can show documentation of where the child is, carefully avoiding biased language or hints of comparisons to other children the same age. Try to talk only about the child's lack of development since your last observation or based on developmental milestones common for children the same age.

Basing Curriculum on Developmental Milestones

Educational decision making should be based on the systematic recordings you have performed. Your developmentally appropriate and sequenced curriculum can be the basis for the program you offer. The program, in turn, is based on developmental milestones for each age and stage of children's development. In a circular fashion, developmental milestones are the basis for the curriculum, and the progress made by individual children occurs because you offer activities based on milestones.

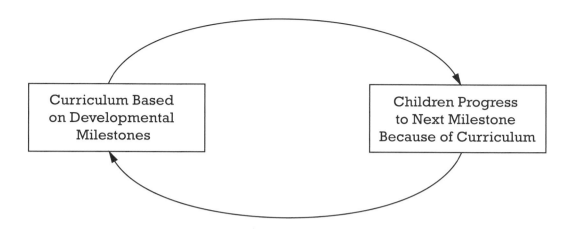

Outcomes can be favorable when you make a conscientious effort to provide experiences for young children that foster the development of milestones. For example, children who are learning to write their names need experiences in holding crayons, markers, paintbrushes, and other instruments long before they begin penmanship. As a caregiver, you provide activities such as painting and drawing with multisized brushes and markers and give children opportunities to "write" often as they scribble their names and the names of their friends on papers of different sizes, textures, and colors. When you observe children to see if they have mastered the skill of writing their names, chances for success are much greater because you prepared the environment.

Chapter 4: Birth through Twelve Months

During a baby's first year, remarkable changes occur in the physical/motor, social/emotional, language, and cognitive domains of development. The developmental milestones that follow in each of these domains are often referred to as *benchmarks of development* or *stages of achievement* and can be identified easily during observations. Typically all babies achieve these common milestones, but they may do so at different rates. Even so, by the end of each stage of development, most babies will have reached the same developmental milestones. Keep in mind that the ages given are approximations, and babies may vary in their individual development and acquisition of skills.

Learning, practicing, and mastery are the three categories included in the observational record. The record provides three opportunities for babies to achieve mastery, though only one observation may be needed. As you observe, record a date and, if possible, a comment when you discover a milestone being attempted, repeated, or accomplished. And enjoy watching the babies!

Physical/Motor Development

Birth to Two Months

Exhibits a rooting reflex
This occurs when an infant turns her head (as if a bottle or breast is available) when her cheek is stroked.

Reacts to loud noises
The infant appears startled or becomes quiet when he hears a loud noise.

Holds head up
The infant can briefly raise her head from the shoulder of the person holding her or from a flat surface such as a crib or the floor.

Makes quick and jerking arm movements
The infant doesn't have a completely developed nervous system at this time and continues to act with reflexes.

Brings hands to face
The infant finds his face and may suck his thumb or put his hands in his mouth for a sensory experience.

Moves head from side to side while on stomach

The infant appears to survey her environment while looking from side to side; this movement is often accompanied by grunting sounds.

Focuses on objects eight to twelve inches away

It has been said that the distance from a mother's arms to her face while nursing is about the same distance that an infant can gaze or focus. Most parents and caregivers also hold babies in front of them at about this same distance.

Two to Three Months

Turns head easily to both sides in supine (lying on back) position

As an infant continues to strengthen his neck, frequent head turning occurs.

Lifts head off surface from prone (face down) position for one to two seconds

An infant often practices this exercise for very short periods of time before becoming fussy or tired. This is another method of building strength.

Follows moving object with eyes

This is sometimes referred to as *tracking;* the infant enjoys watching an object move back and forth slowly. Infants usually like to watch faces more than objects, but know that they may turn away once a face or object has become too familiar due to repeated exposure.

Responds to loud sounds

The infant may respond with startling motions or even crying when exposed to loud sounds, such as a vacuum cleaner, horn honking, or alarm clock.

Grasps and holds objects briefly

Do not confused this with the grasping reflex. The infant will seek a toy and grasp it briefly before letting go.

Three to Four Months

Brings hands to midline while on back

The infant brings his hands to his midline as he explores and discovers that he can control his hands.

Rotates or turns head from side to side with no head bobbing

The infant progresses at this stage from head bobbing to a more steady movement with no head bobbing. While being held in an upright position, she may turn her head from side to side as she explores the environment or hears a sound that is interesting to her.

Pushes down on legs when feet are placed on a firm surface

When the infant is held in a standing position with his feet on a firm or hard surface, he appears to propel himself into jumping.

Exhibits the rooting reflex less often or not at all

As you stroke her cheek, the infant does not respond by turning her head but by smiling or gazing.

Four to Six Months

Lifts head while in supine position

The infant has developed strong neck muscles.

Holds chest up in prone position with weight on forearms

The infant is stronger in the upper chest area and can now support his weight.

Rolls from stomach to side

This is the infant's early attempt at rolling all the way over.

Rolls from stomach to back

This movement usually follows soon after the infant learns to roll from her tummy to her side.

Rolls from back to stomach

This movement usually follows the infant's learning to roll from his stomach to his back.

Stands with support

An infant can stand briefly if you hold her up. This exercise increases leg strength.

Brings feet to mouth easily while in supine position

Infants strengthen upper body movement as they reach for, grab, and pull their feet forward to their face. Doing this also helps them achieve a perception of self.

Six to Nine Months

Transfers object from one hand to another

After taking a toy, the baby can move the toy back and forth at will.

Uses toes and hands to propel forward or in a circle

The baby digs in his toes and hands to move.

Crawls
The baby moves on her hands and knees from one place to another at will.

Grasps small items
The baby uses his whole hand and picks up small toys or objects with his thumb and fingers.

Sits without support
The baby can sit unsupported in a high chair for feeding or on a solid, flat surface for play.

Nine to Twelve Months

May stand momentarily without support
In preparation for walking, the baby continues to gain strength in her legs and lower body by standing often. Usually the baby stands by holding on to something solid, such as a chair, low table, or sofa, and then lets go of the object to take her first step.

Walks with assistance
Babies delight in pretend walking, or prewalking, by holding on to an adult's hands. They may walk briefly (two or three steps) without assistance.

Social/Emotional Development

Birth to One Month

Makes demanding cries
Infants use loud, demanding cries to communicate with us. They may be hungry, wet, uncomfortable, or sick.

Shows sense of trust
An infant's sense of trust shows that he is being nurtured and cared for in a positive way and his demands and needs are being met consistently and readily. Infants often show less tension and more stability when they can trust the adults around them.

Shows attachment (responds positively) to significant adults
Securely attached infants will readily respond to tenderness and compassion from their caregivers.

Makes eye contact
Babies make eye contact for several seconds with caregivers.

One to Three Months

Coos

An infant will communicate by cooing or making gurgling or grunting sounds. Language and speech development are occurring as she attempts to socialize.

Smiles at the sound of familiar voices

Infants are born knowing the sounds of voices they have heard repeatedly while in utero. Many parents read to their unborn babies, and there is evidence that babies "remember" their voices.

Tracks moving persons or objects

Infants have a developing curiosity and are attracted by movement. They are developing their visual acuity during this activity.

Cries to demand attention

Infants are still developing a sense of trust with others, and through crying they practice getting caregivers to meet their needs.

Smiles at strangers

An infant does not possess a fear of people at this age and will smile often at unfamiliar faces.

Three to Six Months

Babbles and laughs to get adult attention

This vocal activity appears to be more intentional at this age as the infant seeks interactions with important adults and other children.

Responds to smiles with smiling

Imitation of a smiling adult or sibling is common. An infant appears to smile when someone smiles at him.

Pays close attention to older children and their actions

The infant watches an older sibling, especially an older toddler, and responds with an occasional smile.

Calms self

An infant can sometimes regulate her own distress by placing her fingers in her mouth or by focusing on something else, such as a toy, her clothing, or a mobile.

Six to Nine Months

Distinguishes voices of important, familiar people
Babies will turn toward familiar voices and give them more attention by staring and moving their bodies in anticipation of communication.

Can distinguish voice tones and emotions
Babies can often tell when others are sad, happy, or angry by the tone of the voice. Caregivers can easily observe the way infants react to these emotions in adults.

Plays games with adults and older children
Games such as peekaboo and pat-a-cake are common, and a baby appears to enjoy the element of surprise, as well as the close interaction with family members and caregivers.

Nine to Twelve Months

Begins to feel anxiety on separation from familiar adults (separation anxiety)
The baby begins to cry or fuss as the family member or caregiver leaves his sight. He appears to notice the absence of the significant person.

Begins to feel anxiety in the presence of strangers (stranger anxiety)
When the baby comes in contact with unfamiliar people, she may begin to cry, cling to a caregiver, or hide her face.

Plays with others
The baby initiates social play, accompanied by laughter and high-pitched squeals.

Appears angry
The baby tends to display anger when he has been denied a goal or the goal has been disrupted. At this age, anger has more purpose and is usually directed at something or someone in particular. Outbursts of slapping, kicking, knocking away, and stomping can commonly accompany bouts of anger.

Language Development

One to Two Months

Coos in response to adults' speech
We know infants prefer human speech to other sounds. They respond to positive speech from adults.

Two to Four Months

Makes squealing and gurgling sounds
An infant learns to express herself through vocalizations. Pretalking sounds are also emotional outlets.

Four to Six Months

Babbles consonant sounds such as "ba-ba-ba-ba-ba" and "da-da-da-da-da"
Although many parents claim their child says "ma-ma" or "da-da" at this age, an infant does not associate sounds with people at this stage of development.

Laughs out loud
Laughing in response to a tickle, smile, gentle bouncing on the knee, and so on, is common.

Six to Nine Months

Babbles sounds such as "goo" and "gaa"
These sounds are a combination of vowels and consonants and are considered to be important pre-speech behavior.

Experiments with vocalizations to include longer and more varied sounds
A baby yells or makes loud, extended sounds when tired and "ahhhhhhhhh" or "ehhhhhhhhhhh" sounds when happy.

Uses intonations in sounds
A baby imitates the rise and fall of adult speech in his sounds.

Responds to own name
A baby will turn her face toward the adult or child speaking when she hears her name.

Develops receptive-language vocabulary
A baby understands simple words, commands, and phrases long before he can talk. His receptive-language understanding is much larger than his expressive ability.

Nine to Twelve Months

Says at least one word
The baby makes a particular sound associated with an action or an object, such as a cracker, cookie, blankie, or shoe. Adults may not understand the sound, but the baby will likely repeat it when she sees the same object.

Gestures or points to communicate
Although babies don't talk, they may indicate their needs by reaching for an object. They may indicate they want to be held by reaching up to a caregiver.

Listens to songs, stories, or rhymes with interest
Babies enjoy being read to and pay attention to music that is played or sung.

Imitates sounds
At this time, most babies can say "uh-oh!" in imitation of their family members or caregivers.

Cognitive Development

Birth to Two Months

Shows understanding that crying brings comfort
An infant whose cries are responded to in a timely manner appears to show a sense of trust that crying will facilitate his needs being met.

Prefers black-and-white or high-contrast patterns
Although this lasts for only about the first three months, most infants show a definite preference toward these visual stimulations.

Two to Four Months

Explores the environment with senses
An infant looks, gazes, mouths, and turns her head to sounds and textures in the environment.

Discovers hands and feet are extensions of self
An infant will stare at his hands and intentionally grab or hold his feet.

Responds to own reflection in mirror
Infants are drawn to their own reflection. They make eye contact and may reach out to touch the reflection.

Anticipates events
Infants begin to recognize that a meal, a bath, or bedtime is about to happen.

Four to Six Months

Shows interest in manipulating toys and objects
The infant is more intentional in making his own selections during this period. He also grasps and holds on to objects for longer periods of time.

Six to Nine Months

Investigates objects by banging, shaking, and throwing
Babies explore cause and effect as they manipulate objects for a desired outcome or result.

Shows interest in objects with moving parts
A baby pokes, prods, rattles, and bangs toys with moving parts as she experiments with them. She also likes to watch moving mobiles and other hanging objects that gently sway when moved.

Shows interest in playing games
At about eight months, a baby can initiate games that are familiar to him rather than waiting for a caregiver or sibling to initiate them.

Nine to Twelve Months

Responds to "no"
The baby can shake her head "no" in response to a question or command from an adult and may begin saying "no" soon afterward.

Waves bye-bye
Usually with prompting, a baby can wave at this age, but he sometimes will wave without a prompt.

Shows understanding of object permanence (that is, knows objects exist when out of sight)
Hide a toy underneath a blanket or behind a box, and the baby will search for it.

Engages in more intentional play
A baby may run a train over a track or place a ball in a basket.

Intentionally selects toys to play with
It is not uncommon for a baby to crawl toward a desired toy, person, or object.

Shows understanding that objects have purpose
A baby begins to purposefully or imitatively "use" objects such as hairbrushes, telephones, and spoons.

Chapter 5: One-Year-Olds

Between twelve and twenty-four months, babies are full of energy and seem to get into everything! Balancing on their feet and eventually walking are marked achievements at this stage of development. Beginning communication skills emerge as babies become more adept at using language and start to develop a vocabulary. Babies constantly seek interactions with other people (peers and caregivers), and as they approach twenty-four months, they develop a sense of self. While the following developmental milestones are common to all children ages twelve to twenty-four months, when you observe, remember that all children develop at different rates.

Physical/Motor Development

Twelve to Eighteen Months

Enjoys clapping hands
The baby claps her hands in excitement or to mimic adults.

Walks with assistance
Most babies walk during this stage without assistance, but some still cling to an adult or to furniture as they venture out.

Begins to use a spoon
The baby begins to grab the spoon from his caregivers, as if to feed himself, and eventually can move the spoon to and fro.

Walks without assistance
The baby walks independently without the help of an adult.

Crawls up and down stairs
Toward the end of this stage, a baby can navigate stairs by crawling but needs an adult close by.

Stacks two objects
The baby can stack two objects, one on top of the other, using her newfound fine-motor skills.

Pulls off socks and shoes
By the end of the first year, a baby can take off socks and shoes but cannot put them back on. He can remove other things such as his diaper, toys stacked on a ring, and objects in a cabinet.

Likes to push, pull, carry, and dump things

Toys that she can push, pull, fill with things, carry, dump, and refill are her favorites. Toys such as balls, trucks, cars, and boxes are great to offer her.

Scribbles without control

Babies will scribble or move an object without purpose until they have motor and visual control.

Eighteen to Twenty-Four Months

Walks up and down stairs with help

A toddler begins to gain motor control and has better coordination as he places one hand on the railing and the other hand in the caregiver's hand.

Walks on uneven surfaces with help

Sand, pebbles, sloping surfaces, and uneven carpets enable toddlers to gain greater balance with the caregiver's help. Falling down is natural, and within a few weeks, her control will increase as she walks without assistance.

Stands on one foot with help

Toddlers cannot stand alone on one foot because their balance has not developed at this age. They hold their arms high or close to their chests to help balance themselves.

Runs reasonably well

A toddler may be a bit wobbly, but he soon masters running (with occasional falling).

Rolls wheeled toys such as trains, cars, and trucks with ease

Toddlers prefer toys that roll and that are easy to grasp when playing. Even or smooth and flat or inclined surfaces are interesting playscapes for toddlers.

Throws a ball

The toddler throws underhanded at first and then progresses to over-handed throwing.

Can feed self

Finger foods and foods that can be spooned are of interest to toddlers. Grasping and pinching are preskills to holding tools for writing and other activities as they grow.

Begins to dress self

At the end of this year, the toddler can usually put on her shoes, socks, and hat.

May begin toilet training

Although toilet training often begins at this stage, it usually is mastered during the third year (age two). Girls generally train earlier than boys.

Social/Emotional Development

Twelve to Eighteen Months

Shows signs of attachment to parents or other family members
A baby may cry briefly when left with a caregiver.

Engages predominantly in parallel play with peers
Babies usually play alongside other babies but do not interact with them.

Begins to imitate older siblings or peers
Imitation is the basis of the role play and dramatic play that occur during the child's third year (age two).

Shows signs of teasing adults
A baby can tease by hiding his face and then revealing it with a huge smile.

Eighteen to Twenty-Four Months

Initiates separation from caregivers
A toddler will wander off from the caregiver to explore or attempt to communicate with her peers.

Looks for "home base" or significant adult
Even though he is exercising autonomy and independence, a toddler still needs to know that caregivers are close by so that he can venture out and retreat as often as necessary.

Plays with other toddlers
At this stage, play is mostly solitary but can include interactions with other toddlers to claim a toy or to make a physical contact as if to say, "hi!"

Shows sense of trust
Each time a toddler asks to be picked up and held or cries because she is hungry or needs to be changed, she is showing a sense of trust that a caring adult will respond in a timely manner.

Shows attachment to significant adults
Caregivers are extremely important to toddlers as sources of affection and safety. Evidence of secure attachment may be observed when a nurturing and caring caregiver leaves the room and the toddler cries or when the caregiver moves close to the toddler and he leans in to the caregiver to be held.

Shows signs of stress when family members initiate separation

Toddlers notice when a family member departs but cannot forecast the family member's return. They live only in the moment.

Language Development

Twelve to Eighteen Months

Uses gestures and actions intentionally

A baby will point to get an adult's attention, hold a brush to initiate having her hair brushed, or wave to say bye-bye.

Intentionally says "mama" and "dada"

Finally, family members can know that a baby is actually referring to them when they hear "ma-ma" and "da-da." Prior to this stage, the sounds were just verbal utterances lacking reference to anyone in particular.

Uses one sound to stand for more than one gesture or object

Early in this stage, a baby develops a sound such as "guh" to stand for "I want that," and then a few days or weeks later, may use the same sound to stand for "That's mine." Later in this stage, he begins to use one recognizable sound to replace a whole phrase, such as "bah-bah" for "Give me my bottle!"

Speaks in jargon or nonsense phrases

Babies use speech that has meaning only to them. It is common for babies to string together vowels and consonants as they point to an object of interest or move toward it. This is known as *prespeech*.

Understands many more words than can be expressed

It is common for babies to know the meaning of more words, especially nouns such as *brother, mama, ball, dog,* and so on, than they are able to pronounce. Some babies do not talk much until the end of the second year, but when they do begin to talk more frequently, they erupt and add many words daily to their speaking vocabulary.

Eighteen to Twenty-Four Months

Says "hi," "bye," and "uh-oh"

The toddler has an expressive vocabulary that usually gets attention, approval, or praise from significant adults.

Begins to express feelings with words

The toddler uses words such as *sad, ouch,* and *mad* to verbally express herself. "Me sad" or "Eva so mad" are examples of a toddler's first attempts to affirm her feelings to let herself and others know.

Uses two to three word phrases

Older toddlers are becoming skilled at putting words together that make sense to them and at getting their needs met in the presence of adults. "Eat now!" and "We go home" are examples of early expressions.

Cognitive Development

Twelve to Eighteen Months

Tracks a toy that is being moved and can retrieve it if it's in partial view

The baby comprehends at this stage that an object, such as a toy, exists even if it is in partial view.

Closes doors

Exercising cause and effect, a baby closes (often slams) doors that are open but cannot reopen them.

Follows simple commands from adults or older children

"Put the book on the shelf" and "May I have the spoon, please" are examples of early commands that caregivers use to engage a baby in thinking, cooperative behavior, listening, and language development.

Turns pages in books

A baby's interest in books will emerge if adults read to him often. Without assistance, a baby will select and look at books he has experienced and will turn its pages, sometimes more than one at a time.

Eighteen to Twenty-Four Months

Begins to recognize colors

The toddler can identify the colors of objects by pointing or touching before she is able to say the names of the colors.

Enjoys container play

The toddler enjoys placing objects into containers and using nesting toys.

Recognizes own image in a mirror

A toddler will smile, pat the mirror, and visit it many times as if to reaffirm it is a reflection of himself.

Chapter 6: Two-Year-Olds

The third year of life is a period of transition between toddlerhood and preschool, and children make much progress in all areas of development. Many toddlers move out of their cribs and into their own beds. They make choices about what to play with, what to wear, and what to eat. They begin to express their emotions and voice opinions. Their physical and verbal abilities increase at a rapid speed, and their need for caregivers to keep them safe is greater than ever before. They enjoy routines such as bathing, toothbrushing, and story time before bed. Peers and siblings are important to them as they continue to play alongside them but not with them yet. Interactions with adults are essential for toddlers to begin to acquire a much-needed vocabulary and become independent preschoolers.

Physical/Motor Development

Twenty-Four to Thirty Months

Rides four-wheeled toys with ease

A toddler can propel himself backward and forward on riding toys.

Runs with ease

A toddler seldom falls at this age unless she bumps into something.

Stands on tip toes

Many toddlers walk on their tip toes or attempt to get things that are out of reach by standing on their tip toes.

Hammers

Toy workbenches are a favorite of many toddlers; they like to use plastic hammers to drive plastic nails and screws. They also tend to hammer with spoons—and just about everything else.

Engages in exercise play

Activities involving running, climbing, jumping, and chasing are popular with older toddlers; boys tend to engage in this type of play more than girls.

Shows interest in toilet training

Toddlers show more initiative to potty train at this age and now, being more physically developed, are likely to succeed.

Opens doors by turning knobs or handles
Areas that were off limits to a toddler before are open for exploration because he can now turn most doorknobs and handles.

Thirty to Thirty-Six Months

Has developed a hand preference
Most toddlers prefer to use either their right or their left hand by this time. Occasionally they switch hands when coloring or moving an object, but in general, they prefer a particular hand for most tasks.

Holds markers and crayons with ease
A toddler shows more interest in writing utensils at this age and tends to "write" or mark on various surfaces, both appropriate and inappropriate.

Uses paint, clay, and dough
Most toddlers enjoy using different media to paint, roll, pound, and sculpt.

Stacks toys with ease
Building blocks, boxes, and other items are of interest to a toddler as she attempts to stack them (usually taller than herself) until the stack falls.

Shows an interest in drawing and marking
Older toddlers make squiggles and draw shapes, such as circles and rectangles, at this stage of their development.

Is toilet trained
A toddler may continue to have accidents, even after being toilet trained, and may still require diapers at naptime or bedtime.

Rides a trike
Peddling is much easier now, and the toddler often alternates between propelling a trike with his feet and using the pedals.

Social/Emotional Development

Twenty-Four to Thirty Months

Shows independence in bathing, brushing teeth, dressing, and selecting clothing
With self-sufficiency in sight, a toddler practices self-care with little assistance from adults.

Is interested in anatomy

At this stage of development, a toddler is aware of different body parts and often shows curiosity in the anatomy of adults and peers by touching or staring.

Has tantrums

This stage of development is filled with emotional explosions when something is withheld from a toddler.

Engages in parallel play

Most toddlers continue to play alone, but they often like to play alongside their peers.

Thirty to Thirty-Six Months

Can identify and talk about personal feelings

Most older toddlers correctly use words such as *scared, fun, funny,* and *feel bad* (among others) to describe their feelings. They can also remember and refer back to times when they felt mad or sad.

Can identify and talk about others' feelings

Older toddlers recognize the feelings of others and talk about their own emotions. Older toddlers also understand some of the needs of others and may attempt to help them or tell someone else about them by saying, for example, "Why is she sad?" or "Who hurt her?" (This is an ability to read the emotions of others, not to be confused with empathy.)

Shows interest in helping

Older toddlers can assist adults and peers with some everyday tasks, such as setting the table for dinner, folding clothes from the laundry basket, and putting on a nighttime diaper. Putting away toys is also a task toddlers are capable of at this stage of development, sometimes with assistance from peers or adults.

Can recite rules but cannot follow them consistently

Although older toddlers can verbalize the rules, they don't always follow them.

Language Development

Twenty-Four to Thirty Months

Shows an interest in print and books

A toddler shows the most interest in picture books (board books or paper books) at this age but also enjoys rhyming books she can recite in whole or in part.

Begins to use private speech

A toddler can use language to direct his actions or intentions and does not require interactions from others. For example, he can say "Jay's turn" as Jay takes his turn without an okay from others. A toddler at this stage of development tends to say what he is thinking and about to do.

Shows ability to use naming words for objects of interest

Toddlers can use words such as *stegosaurus* appropriately if they have a high interest in dinosaurs.

Puts nouns and verbs together in simple sentences

"I do it" and "Her hit me" are examples of toddler expressions at this stage of development.

Thirty to Thirty-Six Months

Echoes questions

Adult: "Where are your shoes?" Child: "Where are my shoes?"

Uses understandable speech

At this age, almost all speech is understandable, even if correct grammar isn't used.

Uses a loud and soft voice

When speaking, a toddler uses different volumes such as whispering, shouting, and speaking at a normal volume.

Cognitive Development

Twenty-Four to Thirty Months

Pretends to read

A toddler wants to hear a story over and over again and may pretend to read it or imitate adults who have read it to her by repeating words or phrases from the book.

Can do simple sorting

A toddler can sort blocks or other toys by two colors as well as sort by two familiar objects—shoes and socks, for example.

Recognizes and names colors

Toddlers learn basic colors, such as red, blue, black, and green, first, but some toddlers easily learn the names of other favorite colors such as pink or purple.

Repeats simple nursery chants and rhymes

Toddlers often chant simple rhymes such as "Twinkle, Twinkle, Little Star," "This Old Man, "and many others they have learned at home and in care.

Sings parts of simple songs

Toddlers like songs that are repetitious, rhyming, and silly. A toddler often sings parts of songs he can remember. He also makes up silly songs that have no meaning.

Shows an interest in shapes

Shapes are interesting and challenging for a toddler to learn. A toddler usually identifies circles first and then rectangles. She can draw circles in the third year, with rectangles following soon after.

Engages in more pretend play

Older toddlers use toys and objects to pretend with caregivers and other children.

Uses the word *no*

No! is such a powerful word. Toddlers use it to attempt to regulate their world and themselves.

Thirty to Thirty-Six Months

Can talk about books

Toddlers can name objects in books that have been read to them and relate the book's story to real events.

Can tell own age

The toddler may recite his age when asked how old he is, saying "I'm two," for example.

Knows first and last name

Toward the end of this year, the older two-year-old may recite her whole name, particularly if her family spends time teaching her this concept.

Recalls past experiences

In conversations, an older toddler often will refer to something that has happened in the past as "yesterday."

Asks questions

"Who's that?" "Where did Daddy go?" and "Where's his mommy?" are typical questions asked by older toddlers.

Creates imaginary friends

Older toddlers often pretend that stuffed animals and dolls are imaginary friends and may name them.

Follows more complex commands from adults

A toddler can follow two-step directions, such as "Get your socks and bring them to me."

Chapter 7: Three-Year-Olds

Now in their fourth year of life, three-year-olds have left infancy and toddlerhood and are now *young preschoolers.* These children are filled with the need to explore their worlds using all of their senses and spend most of their time watching, imitating, observing, and doing. Physical growth slows, and they no longer have the infantlike appearance of a protruding stomach and poor posture. Instead, young preschoolers have a taller, thinner, and more adultlike appearance. Three-year-olds enjoy repeating physical activities over and over, such as sliding, jumping, and riding a trike.

Social/emotional development in three-year-olds blossoms as they engage in silly behaviors and act in funny, precocious ways. With adults and peers as their audience, three-year-olds never run out of material. Children begin developing a sense of humor at this age that make them a pleasure to be around. As language flourishes, three-year-olds explore words and the power they have when used in certain ways. They like to tell others what to do and make plenty of demands. Three-year-olds have favorite words and like to repeat them, making sounds that may be irritating to adults but funny to the young preschooler. They are great storytellers and like to be read to. Cognitively, three-year-olds get better at noticing differences and similarities in real objects, at matching, and at discovering patterns, textures, and lines in the environment. Overall, three-year-olds' wonderment and imaginations make them interesting and enjoyable to care for.

Physical/Motor Development

Swings arms when walking
A three-year-old is much more balanced and swings his arms in a rhythmic pattern when he walks. He holds his arms lower than when he was first beginning to walk.

Jumps with both feet
A three-year-old can now steadily jump up when standing on the floor or jump down from a step or other low object and land on two feet without falling.

Rides three-wheeled toys
Three-wheeled toys such as trikes are a favorite of three-year-olds. By the end of the fourth year, three-year-olds can master them easily if the trike is appropriately sized.

Walks on a balance beam or line
Three-year-olds can navigate a wide beam that is low to the ground or walk on a straight or curved line on the floor. These midline exercises are important for gaining whole-body coordination.

Balances or hops on one foot
A three-year-old can hop on one foot briefly and may change from one foot to the other while doing so.

Slides without assistance

During the fourth year, a three-year-old can climb a small slide with ease and slide down it without help from an adult.

Throws a ball (or another object) overhand

A three-year-old can throw to a peer or an adult (or at a target) but often throws at nothing in particular and then retrieves the ball, repeating the exercise again and again with pleasure.

Bounces a ball and catches it

During the fourth year, a three-year-old can bounce a ball and catch it with more precision than before.

Runs consistently without falling

In open spaces, three-year-olds run more often than walk and consistently maintain their balance, with occasional falls.

Builds and stacks with several small blocks

A young preschooler can build small towers with five to ten blocks or cubes. She delights in building, watching structures fall down, and rebuilding.

Pounds pegs with mallet

A three-year-old can spend several minutes (ten to fifteen) pounding pegs into a board with a large mallet.

Copies and draws simple shapes

A three-year-old seeks opportunities to draw simple shapes, such as circles and squares, or copy drawings of shapes.

Practices zipping, snapping, fastening, and buttoning

Three-year-olds are beginning to attempt these skills but usually do not master them until the fifth year.

Can use scissors

Cutting with scissors is a desired skill for a young preschooler, and by the end of the fourth year, he is becoming proficient at cutting paper with child-sized scissors.

Makes marks or strokes with brushes, pens, pencils, and markers

A young preschooler is beginning to hold and use marking tools in meaningful and creative ways for painting, name writing, copying, and drawing.

Attempts to dress self

As the independent three-year-old emerges, she attempts to dress herself but still has difficulty with shoe tying, buttoning, and zipping.

Begins to stay dry while sleeping

Toward the end of the fourth year, the three-year-old is beginning to sleep through most nights without bedwetting, although occasional accidents may still be common.

Naps less frequently

The three-year-old is typically sleeping ten to twelve hours at night now and may need rest time, rather than a full nap, during the day. Of course, many three-year-olds continue to nap in programs where the schedule is very busy and tiring.

Completes toilet training

During this fourth year, a young preschooler is able to use the toilet as needed and no longer wears pull-up or training pants during the day.

Social/Emotional Development

Shows independence

A young preschooler shows independence when he says, "I can do it myself!" You recognize and encourage his need for independence when you give limited choices, allow him to make mistakes, and encourage accomplishments.

Engages in solitary play

The three-year-old still prefers to play alone sometimes, when using a favorite toy or engaging in a special activity, for example. Her inconsistent voluntary sharing is one reason why playing alone may be preferred.

Engages in parallel play

Playing alongside his peers is common since a three-year-old is sometimes comfortable playing in the vicinity of peers but not directly with them.

Begins to engage in associative play

A young preschooler is finally beginning to associate with her peers on a limited basis, joining them when the activity is alluring and he feels safe with them.

Plays with familiar peers often

Three-year-olds have the ability to pick up where they left off with familiar peers. They spend little time warming up and are able to begin playing immediately in most instances.

Plays with unfamiliar peers

Three-year-olds often play with unfamiliar peers on playgrounds or in restaurant play spaces with a family member nearby.

Enjoys playing with adults as well as peers

A young preschooler seeks playtime with adults often and she attempts to engage them in her pretend play. She might often ask something such as, "Will you play with me, Grammy? You can be the sister."

Begins to show perspective taking

Three-year-olds are beginning to notice the feelings of others and may offer assistance. You can help by pointing out others' feelings. "Shawn looks sad. Let's ask him if he needs our help" is a good way to instill perspective taking.

Likes praise

Young preschoolers respond to praise when you show delight or excitement in their achievements. "You put the toy away all by yourself!" and "Look how you climbed up all by yourself!" are appropriate because they praise the actions of the child rather than the child himself.

Begins turn taking

Turn taking has been very difficult until now, but the young preschooler is beginning to take turns with your assistance. Set up situations where turn taking can be practiced, such as painting at an easel or riding the three-wheeler on the playground.

Begins to share

At three, the child is beginning the difficult task of learning to share. Toys, attention from adults, and favorite objects have been "mine" until now. Take it slowly, and give her a lot of opportunities to practice. Teach the word *share,* and then use and model it often.

Begins to express feelings/emotions in an appropriate manner

At this age, the young preschooler is beginning to talk about how he feels and identify emotions such as mad, sad, happy, and scared. Use these terms often to help the three-year-old recognize emotions and learn to deal with them. Giving a feeling a name can aid the child in her identification of the emotion.

Is happy most of the time

Three-year-olds tend to be happy most of the time because they can self-soothe by playing independently or by asking an adult to help them get their needs met.

Enjoys helping with household tasks

More than at any other age, many three-year-olds delight in helping with household tasks. They love to sweep, dust, turn on the dishwasher, help with cooking, and load the washing machine, to name a few. It is important to allow them to assist as often as possible, whether in care or at home. Their sense of independence and helpfulness can grow.

Likes to be silly and to make others laugh

Young preschoolers' senses of humor are developing rapidly, and they delight in making others laugh by telling nonsense stories. They love to hear silly stories from adults as well and will often imitate the stories to continue the laughter.

Begins to understand some limits and rules

A three-year-old can sometimes be redirected with teaching statements, such as "I know it's hard to get dressed, but we have to wear warm clothes when we go out in the cold. Choose the socks that will keep your feet warm." The caregiver can engage the young preschooler in simple decision making rather than forcing her to comply, even during hurried moments.

Begins to seek adult attention and approval

A young preschooler may be eager to please adults and will sometimes offer to help you by bringing a needed object or exclaiming, "Here, I made this for you!"

Shows fear

The three-year-old's sense of the real and the unreal is not totally developed. She often expresses a fear of monsters and other frightening characters she sees on television, in movies, or in books. She may also express a fear of being left by a family member in unfamiliar surroundings.

Cries easily

At age three, crying takes on a different meaning than when the child was two. He can now use crying as a means to an end—to obtain something or to make something happen. Unmet physical or social/emotional needs are often the reason for the crying. If you can determine whether it is a physical need (related to hunger, exhaustion, wet or soiled clothing, or thirst, for example) or a social/emotional need (related to frustration, boredom, anxiety, sadness, anger, or fear, for example), you can better soothe him.

Begins to understand danger

Playing on stairs or in the street are situations that young preschoolers can understand as dangerous. Introduce the word *careful* and use it often when discussing danger and how to avoid it.

Knows own gender and that of others

Three-year-olds recognize gender and can tell you their own gender. They are beginning to recognize likenesses and differences in the community, including "boyness" and "girlness."

Says "I love you" without prompting

Whether this statement is made in imitation of adults or is initiated by the child herself, she is beginning to verbalize a loving connection with significant adults.

Makes simple choices (between two objects)

A young preschooler is beginning to choose between two objects, such as sandals or tennies. Keep his choices to a minimum for ease and for self-esteem building.

Engages in pretend play

"I'm a big green monster, and I'm gonna eat you up!" The three-year-old spends much time engaged in fantasy play and often enlists adults to play along.

Language Development

Speaks when spoken to
A young preschooler is beginning to understand and engage in the back-and-forth of conversation. When an adult or another child speaks to her, she can give a response of her own. Her responses may make sense, or they may be nonsensical.

Tells stories without prompting
Referring to a child-sized drum, a three-year-old says, "This is my super wheel that my daddy's gonna drive and take me with him."

Enjoys rhymes and songs
As adults sing songs and say rhymes, three-year-olds show more awareness than when they were two. The three-year-old may not participate during the song or rhyme but may be heard singing it later without prompting.

Likes to learn new words
As adults use new words in context (rather than "teaching" them), the young preschooler begins to make meaning of the words and begins to use them in meaningful sentences.

Asks questions
The three-year-old is beginning to ask questions such as, "Where you going?" and "Can I have one of those?" He also makes statements that act as questions, such as "I'm hungry" instead of "Can I have something to eat?" He can respond to questions asked by others with yes or no answers.

Speaks in three- or four-word sentences (young three-year-olds)
"My mom is coming" is an example of a sentence that a three-year-old can say. She may abbreviate her speech by leaving out small words, such as *are* in "Where you going?"

Uses up to seven words in sentences (older three-year-olds)
As they grow, three-year-olds' speech begins to sound more sophisticated and more like the speech of the adults around them. Young preschoolers will catch on quickly and make correct sentences of their own, especially if caregivers model appropriate words and sentences, keeping their language simple and direct.

Begins to use correct grammar (syntax)
Adults can nurture a three-year-old's grammar ability by constantly engaging in conversations with him, using words in grammatically correct ways. Caregivers can talk about things in his world that are of interest to him, modeling appropriate and grammatically correct short sentences (five to seven words).

Understands the meaning of most preschool words (semantics)

Words that are commonly used in the child care setting should be understood by the young preschoolers. Three-year-olds can easily understand words such as *gecko* and *cottontail* if these animals are present in the child care environment.

Uses language socially (pragmatics)

Older three-year-olds are beginning to practice problem solving by (1) making requests ("Miss Julie, can I have a cookie?"), (2) being persuasive ("Will you play with me?"), (3) greeting others ("Hi, Mr. Lee!,"), and (4) giving information ("In a minute").

Enjoys books that have photographs of real things

Photographs of animals and people are a must in the three-year-old's environment. Adults can add to her budding vocabulary by talking about the pictures with her, introducing new words such as *calves* or *goslings.*

Enjoys picture books

Young preschoolers love books about dinosaurs going to bed like humans do as well as books about caterpillars turning into butterflies.

Enjoys singing simple, repetitive songs

Music can assist in developing language in three-year-olds because it is often structured (just like language), repetitive, and predictable. New words and concepts can be developed through music as well as the ability to hear rhyming words.

Cognitive Development

Can stay with the same activity for five to ten minutes (increasing concentration)

As she grows during this fourth year, the young preschooler's ability to concentrate on self-chosen activities increases.

Uses toys to symbolize real objects

At the beginning of the fourth year, young preschoolers are beginning to draw on experiences and visualize them through the use of toy props. Hollow blocks can become cars to drive to the store in. Toy shopping carts can be used to carry pretend food that can be cooked in a pot for dinner in the play-kitchen area.

Engages in fantasy play

"Here's some ice cream" (an adult hands imaginary ice cream to a child). "Thanks" (the child pretends to eat). "You can have the other ice cream" (the child hands imaginary ice cream to the adult). This example of a three-year-old engaging in fantasy play can begin with a prompt and extended as a peer or adult pretends with the three-year-old.

Uses real objects as props during pretend play

As older three-year-olds become more abstract in their thinking, they can use a box to represent a birthday cake or a hollow block to represent a boat, both of which represent real-life experiences that are familiar to them.

Puts interlocking puzzles together

Young preschoolers are moving away from knobbed puzzles and can now put multipiece puzzles together. They enjoy puzzles with pictures of the pieces printed in the puzzle tray, but with around ten to twelve pieces, which makes them more challenging.

Begins to notice patterns

As a foundation for math and reading, patterning is an important skill for three-year-olds. AAAAA or button, button, button, button, button, for example, is the simplest pattern. "Look, Keri, it repeats over and over." ABABAB is a familiar, simple pattern that many three-year-olds can identify. They may be able to extend to the next sequence—red, blue, red, blue, red, blue, for instance.

Can sort or describe objects by one or more attributes

Attributes such as size, color, shape, texture, and number are becoming important to three-year-olds because they are beginning to discriminate likenesses and differences between objects and to recognize the properties of the objects in their world.

Shows an interest in numbers and names of numbers

Three-year-olds are beginning to show an interest in numbers when they say, "I'm three" and "We live at 223 Blake Street." Most young preschoolers can say numbers in order to ten (and beyond) by the end of the fourth year and can count up to five objects using one-to-one correspondence.

Uses words for time such as *yesterday* and *today*

Older three-year-olds are more oriented in time than younger three-year-olds and often use words such as *yesterday* and *tomorrow* correctly (and sometimes incorrectly—"We are going to the park yesterday.")

Uses color names appropriately

By the end of the fourth year, basic color names are often used in context by young preschoolers, and additional colors (favorites) may be used as well. "Look, Mai, you have red and I have red. But I really like pink."

Recognizes name in print

A three-year-old can usually recognize her first name in print.

Identifies and names body parts

Three-year-olds know major body parts, such as eyes, ears, nose, mouth, hands, feet, and tummy.

Uses positional terms

A young preschooler commonly uses terms such as *over, under, above, inside,* and *outside,* and a clear understanding of these words helps him use them correctly. "My ball rolled under that tree" and "Let's go outside to play" are familiar uses of positional terms.

Chapter 8: Four-Year-Olds

Referred to as *preschoolers* or *prekindergarteners,* four-year-old children are a pleasure to care for. They are funny, imaginative, energetic, silly, and often impatient. Their budding independence can be seen in their improved eating and dressing skills. As their eye-hand coordination improves, they develop future reading and writing skills. Their physical/motor abilities also improve and prepare them for gross-motor movements that will continue to develop their running, jumping, hopping, throwing, and climbing skills. Socially, four-year-olds need opportunities to explore, investigate, and talk about the world around them. As they move out of toddlerhood, they rely less and less on adults and enjoy spending time with other children their same age. They sometimes appear fearless, but as they try to differentiate between what is real and what is fantasy, they may cling to adults.

Preschoolers' language improves daily as their vocabulary increases. Culture has a big influence on the words they hear and begin to know. Cognitively, preschoolers are extremely curious and ask a lot of questions. It is not uncommon for them to begin their sentences with *who?, what?, where?,* or *why?* As you care for four-year-olds, enjoy their newfound independence and ability to verbalize their feelings. Each day, they will delight you with their silly stories and ability to engage you in their world.

Physical/Motor Development

Dresses with little assistance
By the end of this year, the four-year-old's ability to tie his shoes and get dressed independently has grown, and he can perform these tasks with much less help from adults.

Runs with ease and stops quickly
Four-year-olds are much more agile than they were as three-year-olds and can run without falling or tripping. They can stop quickly as they play chase and tag.

Throws a ball overhand with more accuracy and distance
Preschoolers can throw farther and with more precision, and they often play catch with peers or adults. They are developing eye-hand coordination as well as their large muscles.

Pedals and steers preschool-sized three-wheelers with ease
The four-year-old has mastered the three-wheeler and has fewer accidents, and as she can turn corners and steer out of the way of objects and peers.

Pedals and steers a two-wheeled bike with training wheels
Older preschoolers are developing physically at a fast pace, and many have graduated to the two-wheeler.

Puts puzzles together with ease

A preschooler no longer needs knobbed puzzles because he is able to use his pincer grasp with puzzles of twelve to eighteen pieces. His prereading and writing skills develop, as well as problem-solving abilities, as he chooses pieces based on colors and shapes.

Copies, prints, cuts, pastes, and paints with a paintbrush

A preschooler can copy some simple shapes and use child-size scissors and glue with simple projects. Her ability to paint with brushes is increasing, and by the end of the fifth year, she can easily hold writing and painting utensils using a tripod (three-finger) grasp.

Writes own name

By the end of this year, preschoolers can usually write their own names and sometimes the names of important friends and family members.

Shows interest in developing large muscles

Four-year-olds are using their large muscles to throw, climb, skip, hop, jump, catch, turn somersaults, and bounce. While they are not as accurate as five-year-olds, preschoolers are much more skilled than three-year-olds. They tend to fall and trip throughout this year, but usually get up and try again.

Social/Emotional Development

Is becoming more responsible

Preschoolers are beginning to follow simple classroom rules such as cleanup, turn taking, and sharing. While they aren't always successful, they show more responsibility than their three-year-old peers.

Engages primarily in associative play

Four-year-olds are very social and are interested in making friends rather than in playing alone. They play alongside each other and with each other but without clearly defined rules or roles.

Has an increasing attention span

Four-year-olds show a growing ability to follow directions and complete tasks, but they still may become sidetracked. They can pay attention for periods of ten or more minutes while listening to stories, singing, playing group games, and cleaning up.

Is developing patience

Four-year-olds are developing more patience and can wait for short periods of time for turn taking, snacks, going outside, story time, or other planned activities.

Understands "boyness" and "girlness"

At this stage of development, preschoolers begin to develop an awareness of their gender and the gender of those around them. Preschoolers often ask questions about gender issues.

Is developing friendships

Four-year-olds use language more than ever before, and their endless chatter needs a target—someone with whom they can connect. Their social nature dictates that they build relationships with friends, if even for only brief periods of time. Friends will often be of the same gender, but not always.

Is becoming a perspective taker

As the four-year-old grows socially and emotionally, his ability to develop an awareness of the feelings of others is growing too. He can read emotions in peers and adults, such as happy, sad, and mad, and can make statements about another's feelings, such as "He is sad because he wants to see his mommy."

Engages in turn taking and in waiting

As a four-year-old reads the feelings of her friends, she is more able to wait for a turn. She can wait patiently as she watches Jenni finish a matching game, for example. With beginning stages of rational thought emerging, she reasons that Jenni will be finished soon and that her turn will occur shortly thereafter.

Engages in group play

Due to his social nature, the four-year-old gravitates to peers in group play. As he associates with peers throughout this year, he places greater importance on being in the same area of the classroom or playground with those he has connections with.

Role-plays

Preschoolers have active imaginations and like to make up stories and characters they can easily role-play. There are no definite rules except that each child keeps her character in play. They often reenact familiar experiences with important adults or TV characters.

Uses words to solve problems

The four-year-old uses words more often than physical aggression to express her anger or to sort out differences.

Shows fear

Four-year-olds begin to show fear of things like curtains moving in the dark, shadows on the wall, or unknown noises. They are beginning to separate the real from the unreal and to learn about danger.

Is becoming aware of sexuality

Developing four-year-olds are becoming more aware of sexuality and may ask questions about likenesses and differences in boys and girls, including physical ones. This natural curiosity is in keeping with their need to question everything and is more about their interest in the world around them than in anything sexual.

May use kiddie profanity

Phrases such as *poo-poo head* can be heard from preschoolers who are fascinated with language and experimenting with the effects that some words can have on adults and peers. Four-year-olds use

Words such as *poopy* (which can be heard in just about any combination) as they seek attention and test limits.

Language Development

Speaks in seven- to ten-word sentences
The four-year-old's sentence structures are much more developed than they were a year ago. An ability to express more complex thoughts, such as "Can we go out to the playground 'cause I brought my new ball today?" emerges.

Sings more complicated songs; enjoys fingerplays and rhymes
Four-year-olds can memorize words to familiar songs with lyrics that are repetitious.

Tells simple stories in sequence
Preschoolers can now tell stories that have a beginning, middle, and end. They are able to narrow the story events to give a logical sequence, such as "They went to the store and then went to the zoo and then went back home." They also use vocal expression and lots of gestures as they give clues about the world as they see it.

Spells name
At four, most children can spell their names, with an occasional reversal of letters. They quickly learn the letters in their names if they have been exposed often to their names in print.

Uses appropriate speech
Although the four-year-old uses baby talk occasionally, his speech is very developed and understandable. He continues to make grammatical errors, but as adults model appropriate speech, he corrects most of the errors by the end of the fifth year.

Follows three-step directions
Many four-year-olds are able to follow three-step directions, such as "Close the book and put it on the shelf and then bring your trucks over here to play." The level of interest in the directions may affect his listening ability or ability to carry out the command.

Refers to yesterday and tomorrow correctly
Four-year-olds correctly use concepts of time, using words such as *yesterday* and *tomorrow,* as they learn to use language for thinking and communicating.

Knows first and last name
Preschoolers have expanded their knowledge of names to include their last names, and many can tell you their middle names.

Pronounces words and sounds correctly

For the most part, four-year-olds can say or repeat the majority of the words they have heard. They may continue to have trouble with sounds such as "r," "th," "f," and "v," but each child is different and may take a little longer to perfect other sounds as well.

Uses pronouns in sentences

It is common for four-year-olds to use and overuse pronouns—he/she, I/me, we/they, and you—as they excitedly tell stories. Instead of saying, "The girl went to the store and got ice cream for her brother," they may say, "She went to the store and she got some ice cream for him." Four-year-olds often leave out necessary nouns (such as *girl* and *brother* in the example) or the names of the story characters, replacing them with pronouns.

Cognitive Development

Begins to reason

Four-year-olds are beginning to reason when they make decisions, understand, explain, predict, and even try to manipulate others in order to meet their own needs. Reasoning often occurs through play, because this is the time when preschoolers practice problem solving. "How many boys and girls can fit inside that box?" "What happens when you hit a friend?" "How much food does it take to feed all the ducks in the pond?" are all ways that four-year-olds try to reason.

Engages in more developed play themes

Four-year-olds are beginning to extend their play themes based on their curiosity and backgrounds. From the traditional theme of housekeeping or home play, a four-year-old is now enriching her vocabulary and emerging literacy skills as she explore themes such as pets, birthdays, the beach, the post office, the zoo, and the farm.

Understands simple concepts

The preschooler understands simple concepts such as age, number, size, weight, color, shape, texture, and distance. Here are examples:

Age: "I'm four but my baby sister is one."

Number: "I have two turtles in my room."

Size: "I'm bigger than my dog."

Weight: "This is too heavy!"

Color: "You get all the brown ones, and I'll get all the red ones."

Shape: "Look at that big circle."

Texture: "I don't want to wear it 'cause it's too scratchy."

Distance: "My Gramma lives a long way from here."

Begins to sort or categorize

The four-year-old is beginning to sort or categorize by attributes such as size (big, medium, little), color, and shape (triangle, circle, square, rectangle). He can sort a variety of objects. As he sorts odd keys by round holes and not-round holes, he is noticing likenesses and differences, a prereading and premath skill.

Puts things in order or sequence

A four-year-old can order objects from smallest to largest or largest to smallest. She can also understand the sequence of daily routines, expecting adults to keep rest time after lunch and outside time after rest time.

Notices patterns

Preschoolers are beginning to notice and identify patterns in their environment. ABABAB and red, blue, red, blue, red, blue are the simplest pattern for four-year-olds and can be readily extended to ABCABCABC or triangle, circle, square, triangle, circle, square, triangle, circle, square. To make new patterns or to extend existing ones, the four-year-old must show he knows how to compare as well as to order.

Counts objects out loud

During this year, the preschooler will be able to count between five and fifteen objects with few errors. As her sequencing skills develop, her numeracy skills increase too. She becomes more logical, knowing that the last number is the greatest one.

Is interested in the alphabet

Four-year-olds know some letters (upper and lower case), especially those that are used in the writing of their own names and the names of important others. They are learning that letters represent speech written down and that words can go together. They are learning environmental print, or print that is everywhere around them—signs, books, and packaging, for example. As they go to the grocery store, signs such as "Apples $1.29 lb" may reinforce that it is necessary to know letters.

Is developing early literacy

Four-year-olds enjoy books to look at and to listen to, scribbling and drawing on just about anything, telling stories to anyone who will listen, and recognizing a few words in print. Reading and writing can come later, but right now, the focus should be on providing a literacy- and language-rich environment so developing readers and writers can safely explore through rhythm, rhyme, song, and text. Reading, singing, telling stories, and writing often with preschoolers will instill a love for literacy.

Identifies colors

At age four, color vocabulary/knowledge is increasing, and he can identify more colors than he could a year ago. He is interested in color names such *fuchsia, watermelon, sky blue,* and *vermilion.* His love for color and wordplay keeps him interested in the whole box of sixty-four crayons.

Chapter 9: Five-Year-Olds

Often called *kindergartners,* five-year-olds develop in predictable patterns, but at their own rates and in their own time. Their developmental milestones are usually met during "windows" or spurts of development. Cognitively, they are incredible thinkers and doers when their brains are stimulated by enriched environments with lots of concrete activities. Five-year-olds are much more self-sufficient and independent than four-year-olds and can make plans as well as carry them out. They make friends easily and enjoy playing simple group games that require rules. Their self-esteem develops as they enjoy success in the many activities planned for them. Physically, they experience a lot of growth in their large and small muscles, which improves the gross- and fine-motor skills they use for playing beginning sports and learning to write. With an ever-increasing receptive and expressive vocabulary, five-year-olds' language skills are snowballing.

One of the most important milestones in five-year-olds is the development of an ability to think about what others are thinking and feeling. This ability is known as *perspective taking.* Perspective taking is a cognitive process. It is different from empathy, which is an emotional process. Five-year-olds are delightful to have in your care—they have high energy and are often funny, full of silly stories, and filled with creative expression.

Physical/Motor Development

Throws a ball to a target overhand and underhand
Throwing at a target encourages the five-year-old to increase his physical/motor development. Many five-year-olds begin organized sports where throwing is necessary, and they develop large muscles as they pitch a ball overhand and underhand.

Catches a ball when thrown or bounced
Five-year-olds increase their activity levels by playing with balls. Catching a soft, safe ball when it's thrown or bouncing a ball by themselves helps kindergartners improve their hand-eye coordination.

Balances well
Five-year-olds walk on low balance beams, lines on the floor or the ground, play structures, and low ledges—anywhere they can practice balancing. Children this age find pleasure in balancing; it is a forerunner to walking and running backward and bike riding.

Uses left or right hand with dominance
By this stage of development, children are showing a definite hand dominance or preference. Although hand preference is mostly genetic, once five-year-olds start using a particular hand to hold a fork, throw a ball, or paint a picture, it is up to adults to permit them to use their preferred hand comfortably.

Jumps over objects eight to ten inches high without falling

Jumping over cones or small barriers in an obstacle course and playing hopscotch and jumping rope are fun activities for children who are mastering their balancing abilities.

Uses large muscles to run, skip, tumble, kick a ball, and hop

Five-year-olds develop large muscles by doing physical activities on a daily basis. Chores or class jobs that can also help children develop large muscles may include sweeping, gardening, cleaning up the block center, and putting away the trikes.

Is learning to jump rope

Most five-year-olds can jump rope independently when they can control the speed of the rope. Jumping with others holding the rope comes later.

Is learning to tie shoes

Five-year-olds are learning to tie their shoes.

Rides two-wheeler

By the end of the sixth year, most five-year-olds can ride a two-wheeled bike without training wheels.

Social/Emotional Development

Takes turns and shares more easily

Five-year-olds are more skillful at taking turns than their four-year-old peers. Their impulse control is improving because they understand time concepts better. For example, they understand that *after* happens later than *now* and that they will get a turn after someone else has finished.

Plays simple games with rules

At this stage, children naturally think up games with rules during play. As they learn more about themselves, their peers, and their environment, they advance their ability to communicate with others. Games with rules can satisfy their need to connect during play as they move from independent play toward group play.

Follows and makes simple rules

At age five, a child is better at following rules that are about things familiar to her than she was as a four-year-old. She can also participate in rule making, such as "No hitting allowed—it hurts our friends" or "Use our inside voices when inside."

Often plays with peers

Five-year-olds are interested in making best friends and often exclude others ("You're not my friend, so I don't want you to play"). Although they sometimes sound cruel, five-year-olds are learning to discriminate between their likes and dislikes in objects, experiences, and people.

Continues to play alone

Although most five-year-olds prefer to play with friends, they also may spend time playing alone, so caregivers should provide a comfortable place, such as a large cardboard box, soft cushions in an out-of-the-way spot, or a "by myself" table or area, for solitary play.

Shows strong emotions

Anger, excitement, and anxiety are commonly seen in five-year-olds. They begin to learn how to deal with these strong feelings with help from adults who talk with them or model ways of coping.

Tries new things without much reservation

Five-year-olds are more daring and self-confident than four-year-olds and are willing to try new experiences. Games that allow five-year-olds to be successful and that are not too competitive are ideal.

Responds to appropriate praise

When praise is used sparingly and is tied directly to an action, five-year-olds respond positively. "You stacked those blocks on the shelf so that they would not fall" is more appropriate than "You did a good job stacking those blocks."

Is self-directed

A five-year-old commonly says, "I can do it myself." Respect his need to be self-directed and to engage in activities that are challenging but that he can master with persistence.

Is sensitive to the feelings of others

Kindergartners may say, "Are you okay?" or "Miss Maggie, Janie needs help!" Five-year-olds are likely to take action when a peer is hurting. Although they attend to their friends' needs more readily, they are often sympathetic to all peers.

Shows strong connection to family, especially siblings

Kindergartners may say, "Daddy is going on a trip to Arizona, but he's coming back in two days!" or "My baby brother is having a birthday party. Want to come?" Five-year-olds are quick to talk about family events and appreciate efforts to feel connected to family while in care.

Language Development

Speaks in six- to ten-word sentences

Five-year-olds speak in nonstop sentences that often resemble adult speech. They listen keenly to adult conversation and, with their expanding vocabulary, can use words appropriately in their own sentences.

Answers questions about familiar stories

Five-year-olds understand that stories have a beginning, middle, and end and can remember ideas from a story as well as retell it.

Speaks clearly and fluently, constructing sentences that include detail

"We went to the museum to see the ankylosaurus" is an example of a five-year-old who has been exposed to elaborate and extensive speech during his life. Cultural values and the kinds of speech she has been exposed to must be considered when this benchmark is measured.

Argues, reasons, and uses *because*

Many five-year-olds are beginning to use reasoning in their arguments to make things fair or to understand the rules.

Makes up stories

Many children at this age create their own stories during sociodramatic or pretend play, making roles or identities for themselves to guarantee themselves a place in the play. Children may say, "I'm the fireman, and your house is on fire. You want me to put it out with water in my hose?"

Converses easily with adults

Talking to adults can be a great way for children to expand their vocabularies and to have meaningful conversations. Five-year-olds can learn the back-and-forth nature of conversation when adults set aside time to talk and listen to them.

Has an expanding vocabulary

The number of words in kindergartners' vocabulary is increasing, and they are using bigger, more sophisticated words appropriately. They may also use kiddie profanity or swearwords they have heard.

Uses language to control

Five-year-olds often need to control activities and peers. Sometimes their attempts to lead are mistaken for bossiness. Children who develop more complex play with rules often try to boss their peers around in search of compliance or agreement. This controlling of others with language is more common in girls and children who are cognitively advanced.

Asks lots of questions

Five-year-olds are curious and are beginning to understand more about how things work, so questions are natural as they try to find out more. "Why do the clouds float by?" and "Where do babies come from?" are important questions to five-year-olds.

Cognitive Development

Counts twenty or more objects with accuracy

After having learned number sequence from one to ten or more, five-year-olds can also count real objects. They must organize the objects in a way so that they won't forget which ones have been counted. This takes memory skills as well as counting skills to do successfully.

Uses measurement terms

Five-year-olds use measurement terms in sentences, such as "That bus is really long," "My bike is so heavy that I dropped it," or "We went to soccer practice at six o'clock and didn't get home until late."

Understands *whole* and *half* and uses them in sentences

Five-year-olds can now recognize a whole pizza versus a half pizza and can use terms such as *whole, half,* and *one-fourth* in conversations.

Matches objects with ease

Sorting and matching activities with real objects help satisfy a child's need to match things in her environment.

Knows some names of coins and bills (money)

Five-year-olds learn and use the names of coins and bills when playing games or pretend scenarios that involve money and when using money in real-life situations.

Estimates numbers in a group

Five-year-olds can estimate small quantities of objects (five to twenty) in jars, boxes, canisters, etc.

Draws basic shapes and more

Drawing may be the creative "language" young children use to describe and connect to their world. They tend to draw what they see (shapes, for example), but they also draw as an expression of their reality (pets, home, the sun, and family members, for example).

Sorts and organizes

Five-year-olds can sort easily when given concrete objects. They are adept at sorting pictures and reading simple graphs too.

Expresses interest in creative movement

Five-year-olds move their bodies like washing machines or pogo sticks because they understand how things move and how their bodies can mimic those movements. They also listen and create movements to music and create movements about their feelings.

Chapter 10: Six-Year-Olds

Six-year-olds are *young schoolagers* who have left behind their preschool and kindergarten years and are now beginning formal schooling, attending either conventional elementary schools or home-schools. In the United States, most six-year-olds are in first grade. They engage in increasingly complex thinking and are task oriented. Their attention spans increase, and they enjoy working on projects and activities that take longer and require more thinking, exploration, and research. Six-year-olds are rule oriented and begin to make up more elaborate rules for the games they play. Their physical growth has slowed, and they have improved fine- and gross-motor coordination and increased muscle strength.

Six-year-olds especially enjoy playing and working with friends. Group play is important to them, and they are less dependent on adults as they make new friends and acquaintances. Their moods can swing suddenly. Six-year-olds use language nonstop and can talk to adults easily, asking many questions. Cognitively, they enjoy sensory play that includes hands-on learning as they manipulate materials and objects. They are drawn to puzzles and model building and like to research and explore ideas on topics of interest to them.

Six-year-olds are individually unique and are beginning to understand the needs of others. Their play experiences are plentiful, rich, and full of curiosity, and their need to make friends is evident.

Physical/Motor Development

Engages in vigorous physical/motor activity
To typically developing six-year-olds, running, jumping, somersaulting, throwing, kicking, climbing, hopping, and swinging are everyday events. As balance and coordination improve, their ability to engage in large-muscle activities will increase.

Rides a bike without training wheels
Most six-year-olds have graduated from using training wheels on their two-wheeled bikes and are now pedaling away. Their newfound steadiness has given them freedom and the ability to continue improving their coordination.

Ties shoelaces
In keeping with the six-year-old's ability to dress independently, she has mastered tying laces. This new ability provides a new kind of autonomy.

Engages in fine-motor activity
Fine-motor activities such as painting, cutting with scissors, modeling with clay, drawing, and wood-working are important to the six-year-old as he continues to develop small muscles and to find ways to express himself through different media.

Writes numbers and letters with improving accuracy

As the six-year-old's fine-motor skills improve, her ability to write is increasing. She is also more interested in the printed word. Some numbers and letters are more difficult to write than others, but the six-year-old practices diligently to perfect each one.

Prints name

Six-year-olds print their names with ease because they have left the scribbling stage of writing and are now proficient at making letters to represent the names of important people and things. They better understand the letters in their names at this age than they did at age three or four, because now they know that letters are symbols for sounds.

Social/Emotional Development

Makes friends easily

During this year, six-year-olds make and often break friendships. They are learning important building blocks for socializing in adulthood while they practice being a friend, solving problems, and developing their self-confidence.

Follows rules most of the time

Six-year-olds develop a sense of security when they have rules to follow. They will invent rules where they are missing and remind peers about the rules to be followed.

Plays primarily with own gender

At age six, it is common for boys to play with boys and for girls to play with girls. Although this is not always the case, six-year-olds do interact socially with peers of the same sex most of the time. This may be caused by the young child's need for familiarity.

Begins perspective taking

Understanding the views (or perspectives) of others requires a lessening of the six-year-old's own egocentric or "all about me" feelings. When a child is consumed by self-interest, it makes him unable to see beyond his own feelings. At age six, he is beginning to take interest in others and to interact socially with them in positive ways. He is practicing the necessary perspective-taking skills he will need as an adult.

Plays in groups

Group play helps young children to get along with others. Through group play, they also become familiar with likenesses and differences in themselves and their peers. Six-year-olds naturally want to socialize, and play is a great arena for them to make the transition from associative play to more advanced, rule-based organized games and sports.

Displays many moods

Six-year-olds are often called moody because their feelings change frequently during play with peers. As they try on many different roles, their feelings fluctuate easily. Usually grumpiness lasts only a short while.

Completely dresses self

Tying her shoes, brushing her teeth, putting on her clothes, and zipping her coat are all activities that the six-year-old can do. The newfound independence is exciting for her (and for adults as well).

Attends to belongings

At age six, the child is much more capable of keeping up with his things. There is much less stress for the caregiver and child when the child can take responsibility and care for his possessions. This is a major milestone for the six-year-old.

Language Development

Uses appropriate grammar

By this age, children have corrected many of the grammatical errors they made when they were younger, such as "He goed to his grandma's house." Six-year-olds communicate with surprisingly perfect syntax (or sentence structure). When adults communicate with and read to children often, children's brains automatically interpret the rules of good sentence structure, and they begin to make corrections to their speech.

Asks a lot of questions

When the six-year-old comes across something she does not know (which is called *a gap in knowledge*), she asks a question to get the information immediately, when she is most receptive to the answer. She will do this from now throughout adulthood, increasing cognitive development throughout life.

Tells stories (real and imagined)

Six-year-olds develop oral-language skills from listening to stories and then telling their own. Some of their stories are about real events, and some are made up. When telling stories, six-year-olds use a variety of voices as well as facial expressions and gestures.

Engages in adult conversations

Six-year-olds enjoy conversations with adults because they can now use appropriate words and descriptions that hold the attention of adults. Adults enjoy these conversations, too, because they are often filled with entertaining and interesting anecdotes or are informative and easy to follow.

Uses language to solve problems

As their vocabulary and reasoning skills increase, six-year-olds are more able to solve problems with words instead of with actions. Their language has become more sophisticated, and their vocabularies have increased enormously.

Cognitive Development

Has an attention span of twenty to thirty minutes

Six-year-olds prefer structured or directed activities some of the time and open-ended activities the rest of the time. They have longer attention spans and can sit for direct instruction in small doses.

Plays games with rules

Six-year-olds enjoy simple rules as they play board and card games with friends and adults. They are interested in fairness and are rule watchers much of the time.

Knows left from right

At age six, children are beginning to know left from right but may occasionally make errors. Some children do not master this skill until age nine or ten, so an occasional mistake is common.

Is aware of time

Although they do not tell time at age six, they are more time conscious and aware of specific events starting at certain times. They may say, "Is it eight o'clock, Mama? We have to get to school." or "Can I watch cartoons at five o'clock?" Learning to tell time may be easier with the use of digital clocks, but an understanding of time sequence is not fully developed at this age.

Is aware of seasons

Six-year-olds know that winter may bring snow and certain holidays, that summer is often hot, and that fall can bring football games and trick-or-treating, but they are not ready for the abstract, scientific concepts of what actually causes the weather.

Counts past fifty

Many six-year-olds can count well past fifty, and some may count to one hundred or more. They understand the sequence of numbers and how they repeat in patterns.

Counts by twos, fives, and tens

Skip counting is common with six-year-olds as they learn to group numbers by twos, fives, tens, and more. One Hundred Days of School is a familiar first-grade activity teachers use to present the concept of one hundred. Six-year-olds bring collections of one hundred items—such as buttons, marbles, small toys, or pennies—to school. They often skip count the items.

Decodes unknown words

Six-year-olds are practicing reading strategies as they figure out the meanings of unfamiliar words, using phonics and context clues, and put them together to read with understanding.

Sight reads

Six-year-olds are becoming avid readers as they understand how print works and discover the value and enjoyment of reading. Their comprehension increases as they read stories and poems about topics that interest them.

Writes stories

As they develop their knowledge of the alphabet and spelling skills, six-year-olds begin to write stories that include things that are important to them, such as friends and family, family trips, and other events at home and at school. Invented or emergent spelling is common at this time and children write words with spellings that may not be standard but that are understood to them. "I lik to pla bawl" is an example of invented spelling and does not interfere with the child's natural progress in learning to spell words.

Identifies familiar money

Six-year-olds enjoy sorting familiar coins and paper money and using them to shop for well-earned rewards. Familiarity with coins—pennies, nickels, dimes, quarters, and dollars—comes from playing games, sorting, and exploring their properties as well as their value.

Knows simple fractions

Children as young as six are interested in taking things apart and putting them back together, becoming familiarized with parts and wholes. Simple fractions such as one-half and one-fourth are easily mastered as children use real objects to discover the ways parts can make wholes. Many six-year-olds will have mastered halves and fourths and perhaps other fractions.

Begins to understand simple addition and subtraction

Now that they know number concepts, or how many objects are grouped with each number, six-year-olds are ready to regroup numbers. Simple addition and subtraction problems with single digits are appropriate, but concrete objects are still important for introducing the concepts. "How many windows are in this room?" and "How many windows are on the door of this room?" are questions about addition that can precede the writing of symbols for the number of windows: 5 windows + 1 window = 6 windows.

Creates and extends more complex patterns

Six-year-olds find complex patterns interesting. They can extend simple linear patterns such as ABABAB to ABCDABCDABCD or even AABBCCAABBCC. They can also recognize patterns in picture books and everyday routines as well as on walls and buildings and in parking lots.

Identifies and draws simple two- and three-dimensional shapes

Although she has been drawing two-dimensional shapes such as squares, triangles, circles, rectangles, and ovals for quite awhile, the six-year-old can now identify and draw some three-dimensional shapes such as cones, cubes, cylinders, and spheres.

Knows the days of the week

Six-year-olds have a beginning sense of order and are starting to understand more complex patterning. These two concepts are important for understanding the days of the week and the way they recur over and over again. Younger children can name the days of the week in songs or by rote, but six-year-olds have gained an understanding of time and how weeks are structured around seven days.

Chapter 11: Seven-Year-Olds

Seven-year-olds have become much more cooperative and sharing, as well as independent. Their individual traits are beginning to shine, and the care and feelings they have for others are central to their being seven. A need to follow rules began at age six, and following them now is even more important as they act more responsibly and take things more seriously. Seven-year-olds now have fears and worries, and they understand more about the world around them and about the concepts of life and death. Their fears often bring anxiety and feelings of dread about certain happenings, such as starting school, making friends, getting good grades, and losing people or pets they love.

The physical growth of seven-year-olds is slowing, with only small increases in weight and height. At this age, boys are usually taller than girls, but not always. Children are generally healthier at age seven than they were in their earlier years, but they still have minor illnesses such as colds and fevers. Motor development continues to improve, and seven-year-olds often excel at playing sports or musical instruments. Their coordination improves, but their physical development lags behind their cognitive and social development.

Friends and family are important to seven-year-olds, and they enjoy spending time with both. Their storytelling and story-writing abilities grow more sophisticated and include better-developed themes and plots. They continue to refine their language skills, which enhance their cognitive abilities and social interactions, and they begin to acquire play languages such as pig Latin. Literacy takes the place of learning language structures as they become better writers and readers and learn new vocabulary.

Cognitively, seven-year-olds gain an understanding of conservation (knowing that a quantity remains the same, even if the containers are different), an important milestones for children at this age. They are still in Piaget's preoperational period of cognitive development and are learning to use symbols when they think about experiences outside of the current experience or in the past.

Seven-year-olds are funny, perplexing, tiring, sometimes demanding, enthusiastic, and fun. They need adults who are flexible and who understand their many moods and feelings, adults who will be there when they need assistance, but who know when to allow them to empower themselves. This is a year of cognitive and social/emotional growth rather than of physical growth

Physical/Motor Development

Rides a bicycle with ease
Seven-year-olds have a keen sense of balance and are able to ride bikes without training wheels or assistance from adults. Bike riding without aids is an important milestone among children this age.

Is involved in sports, dance, or other active play
Activities children choose can enhance their development, and children often choose activities in which they can excel. Physically, boys and girls have about the same strength, but choosing to play basketball or baseball or to take gymnastics, dance, or martial arts classes depends on the child's

preferences and on the likelihood of his success. Body size, coordination, and energy level help seven-year-olds choose activities that are just right for them.

Runs up and down stairs with ease
Seven-year-olds tend to run up and down stairs, jumping over or skipping several stairs and landing with a thump at the bottom. An increase in their motor skills provides an agility they have not had before.

Prints with ease
Fine-motor skills are required to learn to print and do other school activities. Seven-year-olds use their small muscles often to cut with scissors, write stories, and draw and paint pictures.

Social/Emotional Development

Enjoys organized play or organized time with others
Gymnastics, baseball, swimming, jumping rope, and bike riding are a few of the outside group activities that seven-year-olds like to do. Board and card games and projects that require teamwork help seven-year-olds develop social skills as they investigate topics of interest, such as butterflies or weather.

Enjoys solitary play or spending time alone
Just as much as they love spending time in groups, seven-year-olds enjoy playing and working alone. Collecting things, such as trading cards, dolls, coins, action figures, rocks, and seashells, is a favorite pastime for children of this age.

Has frequent disagreements with peers
Seven-year-olds often have disagreements with peers, but the differences in opinion are typically not long lasting and require little intervention from adults or other peers. The emotions of seven-year-olds change quickly, and their need for friendships and to be liked helps children sort out their differences with peers. Seven-year-olds are often impatient, which may cause many arguments to arise.

Can collaborate with peers
As seven-year-olds begin to understand the actions of their playmates, they are able to collaborate and cooperate more.

Plays by the rules
At age seven, children want to be a part of a group and are willing to play by the rules in order to be accepted. As they begin to develop a moral sense, they begin to look at issues in the world around them, such as hunger, homelessness, and war.

Language Development

Enjoys storytelling

Seven-year-olds have learned to think more logically and in sequence, and they can now tell stories that have a true beginning, middle, and end. Their stories are often about real and imaginary things, with monsters, favorite animals, and life events becoming the topics or themes. Telling stories stimulates creativity and imagination in young schoolagers and gives them a sense of pride and accomplishment when they engage an audience.

Enjoys story writing

Seven-year-olds can now write stories that they make up, often with adult help. Story starters, such as word walls with scary words or keyword lists of important color and number words, often propel children to write stories on their own.

Is learning to spell words correctly

Though the seven-year-old once used pretend spelling to write her name and other words, she now has increased alphabetic knowledge and understands that letters have sounds that go together to make meaning. She also knows that a printed word is speech written down. After pretend spelling, she employed invented spelling that used her understanding of letter-sound associations (*b* as in ball, for example) but it looked something like, "I luv mi dg." Now, at age seven, she is more fluent in spelling due to a better understanding of phonemes, or speech sounds.

Uses speech that is adultlike

A seven-year-old uses sentence structures and words that are very understandable to adults. Often mimicking grown-ups, seven-year-olds will use "big" words such as *excellent* or *commotion.* Words such as *family* and *birthday* are often called Tier 1 words, or words that children naturally pick up as they develop and mature. Children also learn Tier 2 words, such as *temperature* and *coincidence,* when adults use them in context or with meaning.

Cognitive Development

Reads with comprehension

Even though they are considered early readers, seven-year-olds are now reading for meaning. Children who have more developed vocabularies read and comprehend better. In addition, children are more interested in reading when they are presented with books that are related to their own real-life, cultural experiences. Understanding printed words comes easiest for readers who can decode or sound out words and who can attach meaning to words as they are read.

Reads for pleasure

Seven-year-olds often read for enjoyment, in addition to reading school assignments. They have usually (but not always) been exposed to adults who read for pleasure. Scary stories and chapter books about animals or overcoming obstacles are popular with children this age. Children who read for pleasure often grow into adults who obtain higher education and communicate more effectively.

Tells jokes and riddles

In addition to being just plain fun, telling jokes and answering riddles can also help children learn to become better readers, to ask questions, and to use abstract thinking.

Shows interest in computers

Computers are everywhere, and seven-year-olds show much skill using them. While screen time must be monitored, computers can be a valuable resource in project learning; seven-year-olds can research particular topics and find information on subjects they are interested in.

Shows interest in maps and globes

Seven-year-olds are interested in geography and use maps and globes to learn about people and places in their community and around the world. Children can also use maps and globes to learn about climates, languages, and world flags. In addition, seven-year-olds enjoy making maps because they now understand that symbols stand for concrete objects.

Shows interest in simple graphs

Seven-year-olds see information visually when they create graphs. Picture graphs and simple bar graphs are easy for seven-year-olds to construct and explain.

Knows months of the year

Seven-year-olds understand that the days of the week recur over and over again and transfer that knowledge to the months of the year and their patterns of occurrence.

Shows interest in current events

Seven-year-olds show a new interest in current events that may be political or humane, such as presidential elections, world hunger, homelessness, and natural disasters. Libraries, videos, and the Internet can be excellent resources for seven-year-olds to gain information on topics that are of interest to them.

Shows interest in history and prominent people

Seven-year-olds have a growing interest in social studies and the people that have shaped their country's government, such as U.S. presidents, governors, and significant events.

Measures objects

Once seven-year-olds master the concept of size, they are ready to take on more specific measurements. Seven-year-olds are introduced to inches and centimeters, and they enjoy using rulers and yardsticks to measure just about anything. Metric and English are the two common rulers that young children use, and although English rulers are most commonly used in U.S. culture, the metric system is considered much easier to learn because it does not contain fractions.

Is conscious of time

Seven-year-olds are becoming aware of what time it is at any particular moment and can read a digital clock and report the time. They can also read an analog clock, telling time to the hour. Young schoolagers are participating in more after-school activities and want to know when they will be picked up from their programs. They rely on clocks to keep themselves informed.

Chapter 12: Eight-Year-Olds

Eight-year-olds are often referred to as *schoolagers* and can be the life of the party! Their outgoing personalities have blossomed, and they clearly are more interested in being with their peers than in being alone. Active eight-year-olds are constantly busy, hanging out with friends and trying new things. They are sensitive to criticism and respond to a firm yet democratic style of discipline rather than an authoritarian one. "If you clear the table, then you can watch TV" works better than "You can't watch TV unless you clear the table" or "Clear the table because that's what you're supposed to do."

Physically, eight-year-olds are full of energy and sometimes feel nothing is too hard for them. Their overall growth is slow but steady, and they look more mature and are generally healthier than they were at six or seven, contracting fewer childhood illnesses. Eight-year-olds expect more privileges, such as later bedtimes. Hormonal activity begins in boys and girls, and mood swings are common. Social competence in eight-year-olds is central to their need to make friends and to be a friend. If their social skills are lacking, some children as young as eight may begin to bully and have difficulty getting along with others. Eight years old is a favorable time to teach children the etiquette skills they need to become sociable.

Eight-year-olds' language skills are well developed, and they are capable of writing and speaking correctly. However, because children's cultures may differ, it is unfair to judge their competence without considering the language they use and understand best. Cognitively, eight-year-olds can manage difficult situations with peers verbally.

During this year, children make progress in the area of concrete operations, meaning they are more able to think using symbols. In addition, they can see things from different perspectives.

Physical/Motor Development

Shows good body coordination
An eight-year-old throws at targets with accuracy and is agile, steady, swift, and strong when playing sports, riding a bike, swimming, jumping rope, dancing, or participating in martial arts.

Shows good fine-motor coordination
At age eight, a child's writing and drawing skills are improved, and he draws pictures in detail and refines his handwriting skills throughout the year.

Has an expanded attention span
Eight-year-olds can sit for longer periods of time (about thirty minutes) but need to have a lot of hands-on, interactive experiences and a schedule that balances vigorous and quiet activities throughout the day.

Shows good hand-eye coordination

The eight-year-old holds writing tools, such as pencils, with more precision and less tension. She can draw straight lines, write in cursive, sketch, draw, and paint because her fine-motor skills improve throughout this year.

Engages in high-energy activities

Playing soccer, baseball, basketball, and tennis, swimming, and doing gymnastics and karate require a lot of strength. The eight-year-old often chooses these sports to burn off energy.

Builds and takes things apart

Concrete thinking allows eight-year-olds to think forward (to build things) and to think in reverse (to take things apart). Computers, radios, phones, video recorders,—just about anything with parts—are interesting to eight-year-olds.

Social/Emotional Development

Engages in group over solitary play

Group play that includes clubs and teams are important to the eight-year-old. His need to be a part of a group is far greater than his need to be alone at this age. Clubs or teams for scouting, swimming, book reading, tennis, board games, cooking, volunteering, music, art, and academics are popular among eight-year-olds.

Is influenced by peer pressure

Peer pressure can be both positive and negative. Eight-year-olds use peer pressure to get others to conform or to "come along" with them. If they urge someone to join an after-school club that puts baskets of food together for homeless children, then the pressure is being directed toward a positive end. But if they put pressure on someone to try smoking, to visit inappropriate sites on the Internet, or to join a group that routinely breaks rules, the outcome can be very negative.

Works and plays without becoming overly upset by results

Eight-year-olds can manage their feelings when they do not succeed or win.

Shows independence and tries new things

For good and for bad, eight-year-olds are curious and will try new things even if they aren't the best for them. As they strive for independence from adults, they sometimes make choices that are distressing.

Experiences anxiety or fear

This is the age when children may worry about things to come and show frustration or symptoms of stress but refrain from discussing their fears with adults.

Plays solitary games

Solitaire, sudoku, puzzles, computer games, and hand-held video games are some of the solitary favorites of eight-year-olds. Screen time should be monitored and card games and puzzles encouraged. Occasional solitary play is to be expected from eight-year-olds, and children who engage in solitary games from time to time should not be confused with children who withdraw from group play or do not have the social skills necessary to join groups.

Seeks love and compassion from others

Eight-year-olds need a lot of love and kindness from adults and peers. Typically developing eight-year-olds are affectionate and want affection in return. They need to trust the adults who care for them and to feel they can take risks without losing the bonds they have with others.

Seeks adult approval

While seeking their own independence, children at this age also seek adult support and approval. They need rules and boundaries and expect adults to set them. They also need praise, but only when it is performance based.

Language Development

Converses on an adult level

During this year, children sharpen their oral-language ability and can carry on conversations with most adults. Sentence structure has improved, and an increased expressive vocabulary enables most eight-year-old children to use culturally and grammatically correct speech.

Adjusts language to match audience

As they use language to meet their needs, eight-year-olds commonly use pragmatics or persuasive language with inflection and gestures when talking. Children use different kinds of speech when talking to peers than when talking to adults. They also use different kinds of speech on different occasions. For example, they'll use more formal speech at a spelling match and less formal speech on the playground.

Uses descriptive language

Eight-year-olds use descriptive and figurative language when they make comparisons: "My dad is a rocket on the basketball courts." They also use similes in sentences: "She swims like a fish." They use alliteration when they repeat initial consonant sounds: "He is as cool as a cucumber." Although they may not understand these terms, they fill their conversations with language that is colorful and imaginative.

Plays jokes on others and loves humor

Eight-year-olds use every opportunity to connect with peers and adults through the use of humor. They play jokes often and use this harmless way of socializing to increase communication and be creative.

Uses language to expresses feelings and emotions

Expressing feelings with words is a developing trait in school-age children. Eight-year-olds are sometimes brutally honest but need to let others know how they feel. Children who are more verbal and those with larger vocabularies have the easiest time expressing feelings. They may say things like "I don't like it when you call me names" or "I'm really mad at you for cutting in line."

Uses slang

Dude, whoa, get out of here, awesome, and *peace out* are slang terms eight-year-olds use to express themselves to friends and peers. Looking "cool" is important to eight-year-olds, who often mimic their older siblings and TV celebrities.

Uses abbreviated language in writing, such as TTYL (talk to you later) and LOL (laughing out loud)

Many eight-year-olds are accomplished instant messengers and e-mail users and use abbreviations such as RUOK for *Are you okay?* BTW for *by the way,* and BFF for *best friend forever.*

Cognitive Development

Engages in projects

Eight-year-olds like to explore real-world events and topics in books, on field trips, and online. They learn best through hands-on activities and like to build models or conduct experiments rather than listen to someone talk.

Uses the calendar

Schoolagers are able to sequence numbers to one thousand and beyond. Making and reading calendars is an easy task at this age. Many eight-year-olds are involved in after-school activities and sports and use calendars to mark weekly and monthly events, keeping parents apprised.

Engages in basic research

Observation, exploration, asking questions, and recording information are common to eight-year-olds. They become interested in particular topics and need to know more. Process is more important than product to many eight-year-olds.

Uses reasoning

An eight-year-old's thinking is more logical and organized, and she needs to know why things happen. She often asks questions to understand the reasons for adult decisions or why things happen in society or the world. Complex topics such as war or poverty are difficult for her to understand.

Shows interest in places and other cultures

The eight-year-old is now aware that the world is filled with children who are like him in many ways but who are also different. Connecting with pen pals, visiting Internet sites with a global perspective, and learning about customs and habits of people in other lands are all activities that interest the eight-year-old.